Dedicated to all of God's children to help them see, feel, and share God's love.

–Misty

God's Love Is All Around
Finding Faith in Everyday Moments
from the collection *Jesus Loves Me*

Copyright © 2025 Berry Patch Press, LLC

For copyright permissions, school visits, and book readings/signings, email info@mistyblackauthor.com.

Written by Misty Black
Illustrated by Gabby Correia
Designed by Misty Black Media, LLC

Library of Congress Control Number: 2025933519

ISBN: Paperback 978-1-958946-16-9
ISBN: Hardcover 978-1-958946-17-6
ISBN: Audiobook 978-1-958946-18-3

Published by Berry Patch Press, LLC. Clearfield, Utah.
First Edition 2025

www.MistyBlackAuthor.com

God's Love
IS ALL AROUND

FINDING FAITH IN EVERYDAY MOMENTS

By Misty Black

Illustrated by Gabby Correia

Jesus Loves Me

God's love is all around.

You can find it in the mountains, trees, and flowers. As you walk in their beauty, take a deep breath, and FILL YOUR LUNGS with God's love.

God's love is all around.

You can see it in the paths of rivers and streams. Like the flowing water that gives life and nourishes everything it touches, God is always finding ways to BLESS AND NOURISH you.

God's love is all around.

You can cherish it with every newborn baby. These little miracles from Heaven help MULTIPLY AND SPREAD His love.

God's love is all around.

You can hear it in sacred music.
As you sing hymns testifying
of His greatness and love,
FEEL THE WARMTH of His Spirit
swelling in your heart.

God's love is all around.

You can sense it in the vast oceans
and beaches, stretching farther than
we can see. The peaceful sounds of
the waves remind you that
GOD IS ALWAYS NEAR,
and His love runs deep.

God's love is all around.

You can share it with the many animals
He created to give you cuddles,
companionship, and protection.

When you love and care for
God's animals, you learn how God
LOVES AND CARES for you.

God's love is all around.

You can feel it in the warmth of the sun as
it nourishes, lights, and warms the earth,
and helps you feel His PEACE AND LOVE.
Each new day is a gift.

God's love is all around.

You can notice it in the little creatures on the earth. Our Heavenly Father created them to spread seeds and pollinate plants, giving you beautiful flowers to admire and delicious fruits and vegetables to STRENGTHEN your body.

God's love is all around.

You can witness it in every sunrise, sunset, and rainbow. The vibrant colors God uses to paint the sky are a reminder of how RICH HIS LOVE IS for you.

God's love is all around.

You can read about it in the scriptures.
He gave us His words so you can learn
about Him and His purpose for you.

He wants you to know who you truly are,
a PRECIOUS CHILD OF GOD.

God's love is all around.

You can share it with the people around you. When you show kindness to your family, friends, and others, you are following Jesus' example.

We feel His love most when we PASS IT ON to others.

God's love is all around.

You can celebrate it because
of the birth of Jesus. He is the
PERFECT EXAMPLE OF LOVE.

God gave His Son to bless us, save us from
sin, and help us live with Him forever.

God's love is all around.

You can enjoy it forever because of the empty tomb. When Jesus was resurrected, He made it possible for you to live again.

By FOLLOWING JESUS, you can find joy in this life and the next.

Do you know where else you can find
God's love?

God's love is found WITHIN YOU—
in your goodness, your kindness, and the
warmth of your smile.

Thank you for being a special
part of my life.

Thank you for showing me what
God's love feels like.

Check out *I Am a Precious Child of God: Mini Devotionals with Faith-Based Affirmations*—a multi-award-winning book in the *Jesus Loves Me* collection.

You can also download free affirmation coloring pages from the author's website by scanning the QR code below.

https://www.mistyblackauthor.com/freebies-for-parents

www.MistyBlackAuthor.com

Social Emotional Learning Books

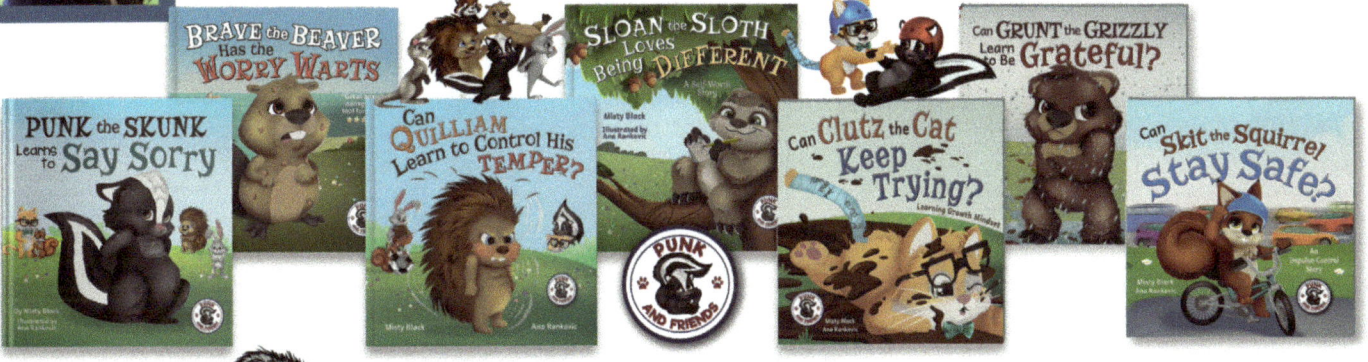

BRAVE the BEAVER Has the WORRY WARTS

PUNK the SKUNK Learns to Say Sorry

Can QUILLIAM Learn to Control His TEMPER?

SLOAN the SLOTH Loves Being DIFFERENT

Can GRUNT the GRIZZLY Learn to Be Grateful?

Can Clutz the Cat Keep Trying?

Can Skit the Squirrel Stay Safe?

PUNK AND FRIENDS

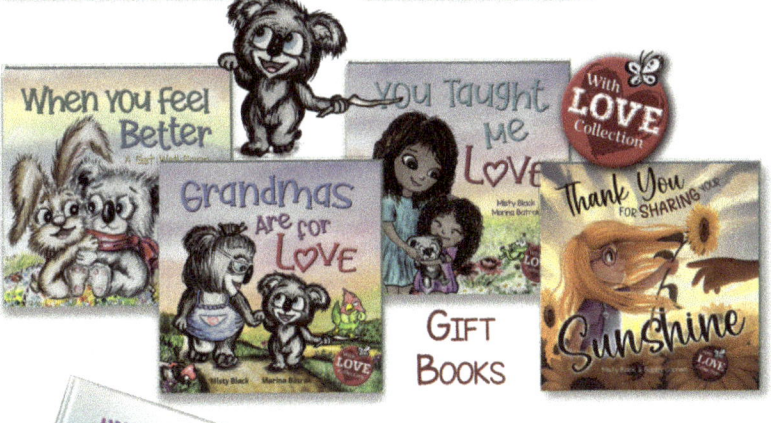

When you feel Better

You Taught Me Love

With LOVE Collection

Grandmas Are for LOVE

Thank You FOR SHARING YOUR Sunshine

GIFT BOOKS

Books to Instill a Love of Reading

THIS BOOK Loves to TRAVEL

READER FOR LIFE

THIS BOOK IS YOUR FRIEND

UNICORNS, MAGIC, AND SLIME, OH MY!

Fizzle Fun

My MOM the FAIRY

FANTASY BOOKS

Bedtime and Holiday Books

Bubble Head, It's Time for Bed!

Bubble Head, HO! HO! HO! Merry CLEAN CHRISTMAS!

Bubble Head, BOO! Happy CLEAN HALLOWEEN!

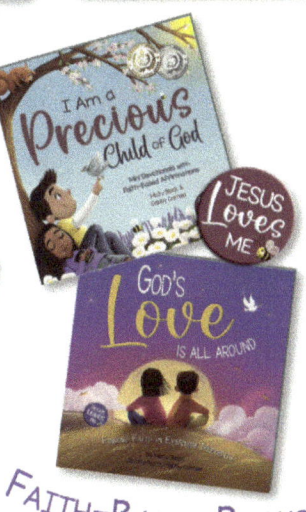

I Am a Precious Child of God

JESUS Loves ME

God's LOVE IS ALL AROUND

FAITH-BASED BOOKS

www.ingramcontent.com/pod-product-compliance
Lightning Source LLC
LaVergne TN
LVHW070121100526
838202LV00011B/330

9781958946176